The Slippery Planet

Rosemary Hayes

Illustrated by Ian New

CAMBRIDGE
UNIVERSITY PRESS

Mark went to the front door. Something was sticking through the letter-box. It was a large, flat parcel and it was addressed to him and Chen. He looked at the stamp. It was very big and it had a picture of a spaceship on it.

Chen came up behind him. "What's that?" he asked.

Mark frowned. "I don't know. Let's open it." They tore off the paper.

"It's a book," said Mark. "I wonder who sent it?"

"I don't know," said Chen. "It doesn't say." He read the title
out loud: 'Space Creatures'. He opened it. It was full of
pictures of weird animals in cages.

"They look very sad," said Mark. He pointed to a picture of
a pink, spotted animal with a body like a hippopotamus and
legs like a heron.

As the boys looked at the picture, they thought they heard a sniff. They watched, amazed, as a big tear slipped down the creature's nose and splashed at the bottom of the page. Chen touched the tear. "That's funny," he said, "it's dry!"

Mark peered at it. "Maybe it was there all the time," he said.

"It wasn't," said Chen. "I'm sure it wasn't there before."

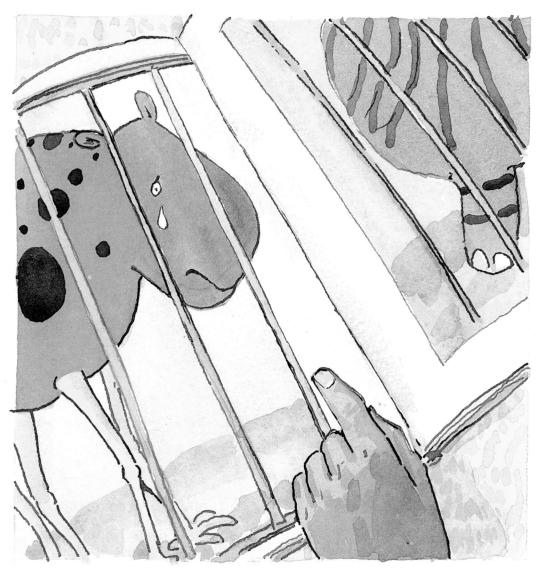

Mark didn't answer. Thoughtfully, he turned to the next page. On the next page there was a picture of a spaceship. On the side of the spaceship was written: 'SPACE CREATURE RESCUE'.

The boys stared at the picture. It was getting bigger. The more they stared, the bigger it grew. "I can see right inside the spaceship now," whispered Mark.

As he spoke, the front door and the hall and the rest of their house started to melt away and the ground began to shake. There was a terrible roaring noise and the boys fell over.

"What's happening?" yelled Chen. "I can't see properly."
Everything was blurred and misty and then, quite suddenly, the

roaring noise stopped and there was an eerie whistling sound.

Mark struggled to his feet and looked around him. "We're *inside* the spaceship," he shouted, "and it's moving!"

There was a big screen inside the spaceship. Numbers flashed across it and then, suddenly, a message appeared:

Welcome aboard! Your mission is to free the space creatures on the Slippery Planet and take them back to their own planets.

The boys looked at each other. "What does it mean?" said Mark.

Chen shrugged. "I haven't a clue," he said. Then he climbed up and stared out of a small, round window.

"Hey! Look at this!" Chen pointed out of the window. Mark climbed up beside him. They were in space and they were heading towards a big pink planet. They were travelling very fast indeed.

"We're going to hit it!" screamed Mark.

Both the boys jumped down and lay on the floor of the spaceship. They covered their ears and shut their eyes. They waited for the crash.

But they didn't crash. Instead there was a slight bump, and then a slither, and then silence. Slowly, the boys opened their eyes. They saw another message flash on the big screen: 'You are now on the Slippery Planet. You will need skates and warm suits.'

The boys found some jet-powered skates and warm suits in the spaceship and put them on. Then a hatch flew open and, nervously, they climbed out.

Mark and Chen stood up on the skates and immediately fell over. The planet was covered with ice. The ice was pink and very slippery.

There was no-one around. There were hills and valleys of pink ice and some strange feathery trees.

After a while, the boys found they could move on the skates. At first they were rather slow, but then they went faster and faster.

"This is great," yelled Mark as he zoomed off towards the trees.

"Brilliant!" shouted Chen, following him.

They stopped at the top of an icy hill, beside the feathery trees. "There are some people down there," said Chen, pointing into the valley.

Below them, they could see lots of strange-looking people whizzing about on skates. The people were bright green, quite small and very thin. They had long, rubbery necks and pointed faces.

"Yuk," said Mark. "They're really creepy."

"Look!" said Chen. "They've got some poor animal in a net. They're putting it on that sledge."

Chen and Mark watched as the bright green skaters took the captured animal to a big, domed building made of ice. Then the skaters and the animals all disappeared inside the building.

"Let's follow them," said Chen, and the boys shot off down the hill.

When they reached the ice building, they stopped. There was no door, just a long ice tunnel. The two boys slid silently along the tunnel.

At the end of the tunnel there were rows of cages set into the ice. Inside the cages there were lots of sad, cold, wet space animals.

"Look!" said Mark. "It's just like we saw in the book!"

"We must rescue them and take them back to their own planets," said Chen. "Somehow we . . . "

SWISH!

Suddenly, the boys were struggling inside a net! And all round them were the horrible bright green people, shrieking and laughing and pointing.

"Let us out!" yelled the boys, and the bright green people laughed even more.

The boys were dragged along the ground.

"They're going to put *us* in a cage!" shouted Mark, kicking and fighting against the net.

"They think we're animals!" screamed Chen. He hit out with his fists at one of the bright green people.

The bright green person grunted with pain, then broke off
a long, sharp icicle from the roof and started to prod the boys
through the net.

"STOP IT!" shouted Mark, but then more bright green
people joined in. They broke off more icicles and they laughed
and laughed as they tormented the boys.

At last, the bright green people got tired of the game. After one more prod and a final kick, they flung the boys inside an icy cage and locked the door.

For a while, the bright green people stayed – they laughed and pointed and made faces at the boys. Finally, one by one, they all went away.

Mark and Chen sat huddled in the net. They were hurt, bruised and miserable.

"Have they really gone?" whispered Mark. Chen nodded.

The boys fought their way out of the net and started to pace round the cage. The walls were all made of ice, but the door was made of metal bars.

They could see a key hanging on a hook outside the cages,

but it was out of their reach.

"We must find a way out," said Mark, leaning against the icy wall. His warm body made a dent in the ice.

Chen looked at the wall. Then he breathed on it. A bit more ice melted. The dent got bigger.

The boys looked at each other. "It'll take ages," said Chen. "But it *might* work!"

They worked all night, taking it in turns to breathe on the ice and scrape it away. The night got darker and darker, and colder and colder, but still they worked.

Then, just as it was getting light again, they broke through the wall.

"We've *done* it!" said Mark. The boys jumped up and down with excitement.

"Come on, let's go!" said Chen.

Mark and Chen crawled through the hole they had made.

Chen grabbed the key from the hook outside. "Please let it work," he muttered as he tried the key in a lock on one of the cages. It turned easily, and out trotted a blue-striped creature like a camel with six humps, trumpeting loudly.

"Shh!" hissed Chen, but the animal was too excited to be quiet.

The boys opened the cages one by one. As soon as they were released, the space creatures started to jump, and buck, and snort, and roll, and squeak, and hoot, and roar, and neigh with excitement. The noise was terrible!

"We must get them away," said Mark, looking round anxiously. "Those dreadful bright green people will hear them."

"FOLLOW US!" shouted Chen above the noise. He and Mark led all the animals through the ice tunnel and up the valley to the spaceship.

"What shall we do?" whispered Mark, looking at the big crowd of animals and then at the spaceship. "We'll never get them all in!"

"We *can't* leave any behind," whispered Chen.

Suddenly, there was a squeal, then some shuffling and some uneasy roars from the animals.

"Oh no!" said Mark. "Look! It's the bright green people. They've seen us!"

Coming up the valley at terrific speed was a crowd of bright green people. They carried nets and dragged sledges behind them. They looked very angry.

"Quick! Open the hatch!" said Chen. "We'll put in as many animals as we can."

But as Mark opened the hatch, the spaceship started to grow. It grew and grew until it was big enough to get *all* the animals inside.

Pushing and barging and squeezing and trumpeting and squealing and roaring, the animals stampeded into the spaceship. Chen followed them, and Mark was just jumping in after him when the bright green people whizzed up to the spaceship.

They grabbed Mark's legs and pulled him hard, but Chen hung on to his arms. Then, with a roar, the spaceship started to move, the hatch closed, and they were off.

Inside the spaceship, there was a terrible noise and a lot of stamping and bumping.

"We're going to get squashed!" yelled Chen.

Just then, the spindly-legged hippo knelt down beside them and they climbed onto its back. From there they could see the screen. On the screen was a map showing lots of planets, and on each planet was a picture of a space creature.

They dropped off the animals one by one on their own
planets. Every animal said a noisy 'thank you' as it left
the spaceship.

The last planet they visited was big with pink stripes. The
camel with six humps jumped out. Mark and Chen waved
from the window and watched it trot happily away.

"Phew!" said Mark. "We've done it!"

As he spoke, the spaceship started to change. At first, things became blurred and misty. Then, very slowly, they could see properly again. The boys blinked and rubbed their eyes. They were standing in the hall by the front door.

"We're back home!" said Mark. He was still holding the book. Chen turned the pages. "Look!" he said. "The animals aren't in cages any more. They're on their own planets!"

"And they don't seem sad now," said Mark. Then he turned to the picture of the spaceship . . .

"Wow!" said Chen. "Look who's in the spaceship!"
The boys stared in disbelief at what they saw.